Sports History

The Story of Figure Skating

Anastasia Suen

The Story of Figure Skating
Copyright © 2001 by Rosen Book Works, Inc.

On Deck® Reading Libraries
Published by Rigby
1000 Hart Road
Barrington, IL 60010-2627
www.rigby.com

Book Design: Laura Stein
Text: Anastasia Suen
Photo Credits: Front cover, p.11 © Underwood & Underwood/Corbis;
p. 5 © Dave Bartuff/Corbis; pp. 6–7, 14 (inset), 18–19 © Bettman/
Corbis; p. 9 © Library of Congress; p.10 © Archive Photos; p.12, back
cover © Duomo/Corbis; p.13 © The United States Figure Skating Museum;
pp.14–15 © Hulton-Deutsch Collection/Corbis; p.17 © Hulton Getty/
Archive Photos; p. 21 © Reuters/Blake Sell/Archive Photos

On Deck® is a trademark of Reed Elsevier Inc. registered
in the United States and/or other jurisdictions

07 06 05
10 9 8 7 6 5 4 3

Printed in China

ISBN 0-7635-7855-X

Contents

The Beginning

People have been skating on ice for thousands of years. The blades of the earliest skates were made from animal bones. Later, the blades were made from metal.

IT'S A FACT!

In the Netherlands, a skeleton of a person from 10,000 B.C. was found with animal bone blades tied to the feet.

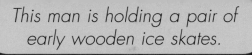

This man is holding a pair of early wooden ice skates.

5

Figure Skating in Europe

In Europe, people skated for fun. They used their skates to draw shapes, called figures, on the ice. This became known as figure skating.

People have been ice-skating on frozen lakes for many years.

Many skating clubs were formed in the 1800s. Contests were held to see who could make the best figures on the ice.

Dancing on Ice

People in the United States also liked to figure skate. In the 1860s, an American dancer named Jackson Haines changed the way people figure skated. He added many dance moves to his skating.

Jackson Haines

Jackson Haines also changed the ice skate. He made the blades part of the boots. Before this change, blades were tied to skaters' shoes. Haines' invention made it easier to dance and spin on the ice.

Early ice-skaters tied metal blades to their shoes.

Ice-skaters can move better when the blades are part of the skater's shoe.

In the 1870s, new skates had toe picks on the tips of the blades. Toe picks are tiny teeth that help skaters jump and spin.

Toe pick

Toe picks stick in the ice so skaters can have more control over their moves.

Axel Paulsen used skates with toe picks to create a new move. He jumped high and landed backward after spinning around in the air. This jump is called an axel.

These skaters in the late 1800s enjoyed a day on the ice in Central Park in New York City.

In 1896, the first world figure skating championship was held in Saint Petersburg, Russia. Skating had become popular around the world.

Skating champions traveled from all over the world to compete in Saint Petersburg.

The Olympics

In 1924, figure skating was an event in the first winter Olympic Games. In 1928, Sonja Henie from Norway won the women's gold medal for skating. She was only fifteen years old.

Total Number of Olympic Gold Medals Won

Great Britain	U.S.A.	Russia
5	12	19

Sonja Henie was the first ice-skater to wear a short skirt. It let her move more freely.

Dick Button was an Olympic skater who changed figure skating with his exciting style. Fans loved to see him do triple jumps and double axels.

Dick Button was the first skater to do a triple jump in the Olympics.

Many people love to figure skate.
Millions of fans watch figure skaters
on television and at live events.
Figure skating is a lively and
fun sport.

Tara Lipinski won the Olympic gold medal when she was only fifteen years old.

Glossary

championship (**cham**-pea-uhn-shihp) a contest that decides the best participant in a sport

compete (kuhm-**peet**) to try hard to win a contest

contests (**kahn**-tehsts) games to see who is better at something

figure (**fihg**-yuhr) a shape or pattern drawn on ice with ice skates

skeleton (**skehl**-uh-tuhn) the bones inside the body of a person or animal

Resources

Books

This Is Figure Skating
by Margaret Blackstone
Henry Holt and Company (1998)

Young Ice Skater
by Peter Morrissey
Dorling Kindersley Publishing (1998)

Web Site

Figure Skating Photographs
http://www.icepix.com

Index